Chinese Quick Guides

ESSENTIAL CHINESE CHARACTERS: A CULTURAL GUIDE

Brenda Yaxin Qian

LONG RIVER PRESS
San Francisco

Author: Brenda Yaxin Qian
Edition Editor: Lily Lijuan Zhou
Cover Design & Layout: SinoMedia Ltd.
Illustrations: Fu Jie
Publisher: Zhang Ruizhi & Xu Mingqiang

First Edition July 2005

ISBN 1-59265-045-7

Published in the United States of America by
Long River Press
360 Swift Ave., Suite 48, South San Francisco, CA 94080
www.longriverpress.com
in association with Haiwen Audio-Video Publishers

Printed in China

Introduction

This book is dedicated to readers who are interested in the Chinese language and its culture and enjoy learning some Chinese characters. The Chinese language is one of the oldest languages in the world. Its unique characters bear profound cultural connotations.

In this book the author selected 36 characters, all of which are frequently used in modern Chinese language, most of which are characters of Chinese virtues and are deeply immersed in the culture. For each character the author first analyzed its structure and then proceeded to explain its evolution of form and meaning. The focus however is on explaining the cultural connotation, trying to unknot the close tie between its original meaning and cultural influences. A list of frequently used phrases was appended at the end of each chapter.

The main purpose of the book is to help foreign Chinese learners better understand Chinese characters and its connection with the Chinese culture.

Brenda Qian

Contents

Bone script (甲骨文)

Bone script (*Jiaguwen*) refers to the script carved by the ancients of the Shang Dynasty (c.16th – 11th century BC) on tortoise shells and animal bones. It is considered to be the earliest written language of China.

Bronze script (金文)

Bronze script (*Jinwen*) refers to the script cast or carved on ancient bronze objects in Shang (c.16th – 11th century BC) and Zhou Dynasties (c. 11th century – 256BC). *Jinwen* literally means the script carved on the metal.

Seal script (篆书)

Seal script in this book refers to Small Seal Script (*Xiaozhuan*). It came into being when Emperor Qin Shihuang of Qin Dynasty (221BC – 206BC) unified the whole China under one central government and unified different systems of written language into a simplified one.

Regular script (楷书)

Regular script (*Kaishu*), developed in Wei (220 – 265) and Jin Dynasties (265 – 420) is square in form, non-cursive in style, more simplified and easier to write. It is used even today as a standard form of writing.

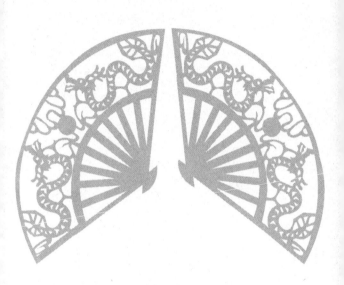

福 fú blessing

福 is used most of the time as a noun, meaning "good fortune", "blessing" and "happiness". The original meaning for 福 is "praying to god for blessing". It evolved to mean "the god-blessed state of life or happiness" in general.

丶	冫	礻	礻	祄	祄	祈
祒	祒	禞	禞	福	福	

Evolution of form:

In the bone script 福 is written as ![bone script], the left bottom
part symbolizes both hands, above them is a vase of wine,
the right radical indicates an official sacrifice service.

bronze script 福 **seal script** 祖

regular script 福

Cultural connotation:

福 is really a desired mental and physical state during one's life as opposed to 祸(huò misfortune). It indicates a state filled with wealth, fortune, happiness and god's blessing. During the Chinese spring festival, many Chinese families would stick a red paper with the character 福 upside down on their doors. (倒，means "upside down" is the homonym to 到，which means "arrive, reach" in Chinese). This is supposed to mean that in the coming year they would be overwhelmed by 福.

Frequently used phrases:

享(xiǎng enjoy)福: enjoy the ease and comfort of life

发(fā develop)福: a nice way of telling people who have gained weight

福气(qì luckiness): good fortune

祝(zhù wish)福: blessing; wish

福利(lì profit): welfare; well-being

福如(rú like)东(dōng east)海(hǎi sea): a term of congratulations on old people's birthday, meaning happiness is as boundless as the eastern sea

寿 shòu **longevity**

寿 is used as a noun meaning "long life", "old people's birthday". It is also an euphemism for a funeral. The original meaning was "aging". It has later come to mean "longevity", "life-span", "birthday", and so on.

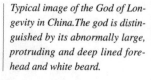

Typical image of the God of Longevity in China. The god is distinguished by its abnormally large, protruding and deep lined forehead and white beard.

| 一 | 二 | 三 | 丰 |
| 丰 | 寿 | 寿 | |

Evolution of form:

In the bone script 寿 is written as ![]. This character has many variants in ancient times, but its basic construction was 老 (indicating its meaning) and 疇 (indicating its sound).

7

***Cultural connotation*:**

寿 means long life and in the old days when very few people would live up to seventy years old, long life was almost the synonym of bliss. When people die at a really advanced age it is considered a good thing and their bodies would be wrapped up in shrouds that Chinese people call "shòu yī(寿衣)". When an elderly person's birthday is celebrated, his or her family would address him or her as "shòu xīng" and prepare many "shòu táo(寿桃 peach)" and "shòu miàn(寿面 noodle)" to share with the guests.

Frequently used phrases:

寿星(xīng star): a senior whose birthday is being celebrated

寿面(miàn noodle):birthday noodles for the meaning of longevity

长(cháng long)寿: longevity

寿比(bǐ compare)南山(nánshān Zhongnan Mountain): may you live to be as old as Zhongnan Mountain

9

缘 yuán predestined relationship

缘 is used either as a noun or a preposition. Originally it only referred to the frills on clothes. Gradually it has evolved to mean "border of the clothes", then "border" by itself, then "go along the border" when used as a preposition. However, the most important meaning of 缘 is "predestined relationship".

| L | 幺 | 乡 | 纟 | 纾 | 终 |
| 纱 | 终 | 绉 | 缘 | 缘 | 缘 |

Evolution of form:

缘 was invented quite late so only its seal script is available. As 緣 is a phonogram, its meaning goes after the radical on the left, its sound after the right part. In the seal script, the left part radical is written as 糸 , symbolizing "silk thread on the fabric".

Cultural connotation:

Most Chinese people believe in the importance of 缘 and would often regard it as one of the key factors in a relationship. If two people are said to have predestined 缘 they are very likely to become good friends or successful partners. If a boy and girl are said to have predestined 缘, they are likely to get married and live happily together for the rest of their lives. Conversely if a couple doesn't own this predestined 缘, their love will go through many hardships and is very likely to end sadly at some point. Actually 缘 sometimes functions as a psychological hint. For example, if two people get along really well, both would think that they are probably predestined to be friends, therefore both would take the friendship more seriously and be more dedicated to it. If two people do not get along then either one would suppose they don't have any 缘 to be together anyway, thus both are free from blaming themselves or the other person.

Frequently used phrases:

缘分(fèn affection): fate or chance that brings people together

姻(yīn marriage)缘: predestined marital relationship

缘故(gù reason): reason; cause

喜(xǐ happiness)结(jié form; tie)良(liáng good)缘: consummate a marriage happily

有(yǒu have)缘千里(qiānlǐ a thousand *li* away)来(lái come)相会(xiānghuì meet): people living far apart will meet if they are destined to

Do you know?

Chinese Cupid (Yuèlǎo)

In Chinese legend, there is the God of Marriage, who is a kind old man with a magic red thread in his hand. It is said that if he ties the thread between a man and a woman, they are destined to become a couple. That explains why in a traditional

Chinese marriage ceremony, the bride and bridegroom would hold a red cloth together. The God is known as 月老 (Yuèlǎo an old man in the moon) and is as well-known in China as Cupid is in Western countries.

喜 Xǐ **happiness**

喜 is used either as a noun or a verb. As a verb it means "be delighted" or "have an inclination for"; as a noun it means "a happy event", "an occasion for celebration".

一	十	士	壮	吉	吉
吉	吉	壴	亳	喜	喜

Evolution of form:

In the bone script 喜 is written as 豈. This character is composed of two parts, "壴" and "口". "壴" stands for "鼓" meaning "drum", and "口" images a smiling mouth. The two parts, put together, indicate a very happy occasion on which people laugh and beat drums.

bronze script 喜 **seal script** 喜 **regular script** 喜

Cultural connotation:

In China, people generally classify one's life into times of sadness and times of happiness. 喜 refers to times of happiness and according to a poet from the Song Dynasty there are four major events considered to be the happiest moments during a person's life in China. They are namely the moments when one gets married, when one is enrolled in advanced education, when one meets an old friend in a foreign land and when a timely rain falls after a long drought. Among these four happy events marriage ranks above the other three and 喜 is often seen in wedding terms. On the day of a wedding banquet you will see the new couple's house and car and the restaurant where the banquet is held decorated with numerous "double-happiness" red paper cuts in the shape of two combined 喜 characters. Besides there are some other events that would be considered 喜 in China, such as moving to a new house, opening a new store, the delivery of a baby and the news that your friend or relative's wife is pregnant.

Frequently used phrases:

喜糖(táng sweets): wedding candies

喜酒(jiǔ wine): wedding banquet

喜剧(jù drama): comedy

喜鹊(què magpie): magpie

喜悦(yuè happy): delightful; happy

有(yǒu have)喜: be pregnant

双(shuāng both)喜临门(línmén arrive at the door): a double blessing has descended upon the house

喜出(chū go beyond)望(wàng hope; wish)外(wài beyond): be overjoyed (at unexpected good news, etc.)

喜怒(nù anger)哀(āi grief)乐(lè joy): the whole gamut of sentiments

爱 ài love

爱 is mostly used as a verb meaning "love" or "cherish". Although its original meaning was "bestow favors on", it gradually developed the meaning of "cherish" and "love".

爱（愛）

| 一 | 一 | 一 | 爫 | 爫 |
| 爫 | 爫 | 受 | 旁 | 爱 |

Evolution of form:

bone script    bronze script

seal script   regular script 爱

Cultural connotation:

Although translated into "love", its cultural connotation is slightly different from the English word. In Western culture, love is more associated with passion and sexual desire which brings pleasure and satisfaction. However, in traditional Chinese culture, sexual appeal between men and women is despised as a loss of virtue. In a lot of cases love was kept secret, therefore it brings not pleasure but sacrifice and sadness. Paradoxically since love is so hard and sometimes even excruciating, it seems truly pure and dear to people nowadays.

Frequently used phrases:

爱人(ren person): husband / wife

爱好(hào like): hobby

爱情(qíng emotion): love

爱心(xīn heart): love; sympathy; compassion

博(bó abundant)爱: universal love; universal fraternity

爱不(bú not)释(shì let go)手(shǒu hand): be so fond of something that one can hardly put it down

爱屋(wū house)及(jí extend)乌(wū crow): love me, love my dog

Do you know?

Butterfly Lovers
(Chinese Romeo and Juliete)

When we talk about the word "love", we can't miss the well-known tragic love story of Liang Shanbo and Zhu Yingtai. The two loved each other whole-heartedly, but like Shakespeare's Romeo and Juliete, their love didn't lead  to a happy ending. As Liang was from a poor family, Zhu's parents wouldn't accept him and arranged to marry their daughter to a rich man. Liang was prevented from meeting Zhu and later died because he missed her so much. When Zhu learned the news, she escaped from the arranged wedding ceremony and ran to Liang's tomb. There she cried with a broken heart and hit the tombstone with her head killing herself. God was moved by their devoted love and magically turned them into butterflies so they could be together in the sky.

德 dé morals

德 is a noun meaning "virtue" or "morals". The bone script of this character features a foot on the left 彳 representing any behavior and an eye with a vertical line on the right 𡇡 signifying looking straight ahead. In the very early days virtue or morals means one could look straight ahead with a clear conscience.

`	⸗	彳	彳	彳	彳	彳	彳
彳	彳	彳	德	德	德	德	

Evolution of form:

bone script 𝍿 bronze script 德

seal script 德 regular script 德

Cultural connotation:

In China the status of morality is equal to the law. It is a nobler pursuit to be a virtuous person than simply a law-abiding person. Children educated at Chinese schools are not only taught knowledge, but are also required to learn what morality is and their responsibilities as a moral person. In the eyes of most Chinese people an excellent person should not only have talent and knowledge but also integrity. And in the eyes of ancient Chinese rulers, morality and virtue outweighs the possession of land, people or wealth. Confucius once taught **"The ruler must first take pains about his own virtue. Possessing virtue will give him the people. Possessing the people will give him the territory. Possessing the territory will give him its wealth. Possessing the wealth, he will have resources for expenditure. Virtue is the root; wealth is the result."**

Frequently used phrases:

德育(yù education): moral education

道(dào morality)德: morality; ethics

品(pǐn character)德: moral character

德才(cái ability; talent)兼备(jiānbèi have both…and…): have both ability and integrity

德高(gāo of a high degree)望(wàng prestige)重(zhòng considerable in amount or value): (of an old person) be of noble character and high prestige

德智(zhì intelligence)体(tǐ body)全面(quánmiàn comprehensive)发展(fāzhǎn development): *(slogan popular in Chinese elementary and middle schools)* all round development of morality, intelligence and physique

忠 zhōng loyal

忠 is an adjective meaning "loyal" and "devoted". It is a phonograph. Its sound follows the character of 中 and its meaning follows the heart below .

(see page 34)

30

丶	冖	口	中
忠	忠	忠	忠

Evolution of form:

The simplified regular script of 忠 derives directly from
its bronze script written as 𢜩.

Cultural connotation:

Chinese people traditionally value loyalty above other qualities, particularly during the feudal period. When the great general Yue Fei in the Southern Song Dynasty was captured by his enemies, they revealed the tattoo on his back —Loyal to My Motherland（精忠报国）. Loyalty is not only expected of gentlemen and heroes, it is also expected of women. Once a woman is married to a man she is supposed to stay with him regardless of any change.

Frequently used phrases:

忠厚(hòu kind; magnanimous): honest and tolerant, sincere and kind

忠贞(zhēn loyal; faithful): loyal and steadfast

忠诚(chéng sincerity): loyal; faithful

忠心(xīn heart): faithful and righteous

忠告(gào advice): sincere advice; exhortation

忠言(yán speech; word)逆耳(nì'ěr grate on the ear;
unpleasant to hear): good advice jars on the ear

忠于(yú to; concerning)职守(zhíshǒu post; duty): be
faithful in the discharge of one's duties

Do you know?

Yue Fei's Tattoo

Yue Fei (1103-1141) was the great patriotic hero in China's history and his memorial temples have become famous scenic spots in China. As the tattoo (Loyalty to My Motherland) on his back shows, Yue Fei is regarded as the symbol of loyalty among Chinese. It is said that the tattoo was carved by Yue Fei's mother the night before he joined the army. She expressed her wish for Yue Fei to devote his life to safeguard their motherland instead of worrying about the family. As a filial young man, Yue Fei bore his mother's words in mind and became a famous general in the Southern Song Dynasty. The story of "Yue's Mother Carving Tattoo" has then spread widely.

忍 rěn **tolerate**

忍 is used as a verb meaning "be patient" and "tolerate". The original meaning and shape of the character suggest

that to tolerate is to hold a knife 刃 above your heart 心 .

(see page 39)

忍

| フ | 刀 | 刃 | 刃 |
| 忍 | 忍 | 忍 | |

Evolution of form:
bronze script 忍 **regular script** 忍

36

Cultural connotation:

Influenced by Buddhist spirits Chinese people generally value patience and tolerance as a precious quality. In fact most of the great names in history had to face setbacks with great patience and tolerance. It gives people the calmness to deal with complicated situations and the strength to survive through difficult times. However, tolerance is a different word from timidity. Although Chinese people are very tolerant by tradition they are by no means lacking in backbone. When driven to the limits of tolerance, they will stand up to defend themselves.

Frequently used phrases:

容(róng tolerate)忍: put up with

忍辱(rǔ humiliation)负(fù bear)重(zhòng weight):
endure humiliation in order to carry out an important
mission

忍痛(tòng pain)割(gē cut)爱(ài cherish): part reluc-
tantly with what one treasures

忍无(wú not)可(kě can; may)忍: be driven beyond
the limits of forbearance

小(xiǎo small)不(bù not)忍则(zé conjunction)乱
(luàn confuse)大(dà big)谋(móu scheme): lack of
forbearance in small matters upsets or spoils great plans

Do you know?

Story of General Han Xin

Han Xin was a military talent who contributed greatly to the establishment of the Han Dynasty (206BC-AD220). But when he was young, he experienced unbelievable humiliation. As a young man of great ambition, Han Xin studied military strategies. But since he was from a poverty-stricken family, he was looked down upon by rich men in his neighborhood. One day they surrounded Han Xin and a big guy said provokingly to him "I bet you're a coward. Dare you kill me with the sword in your hand? If not, creep through my crotch!" Han Xin knew that if he thrust the man, the rascals would kill him and all his ambitions and efforts would end in vain. He kept calm and chose to endure the humiliation for his future. This is the famous story of "Humiliation under Crotch" and is always cited to show the importance of tolerance. People are impressed with Han Xin's tolerance and admire him for his great achievements as a military general.

慧 huì intelligent

慧 is an adjective meaning "intelligent, talented" or "wise". Originally it was borrowed as a Buddhism term, meaning "completely aware of" (了悟). Later the meaning extended to mean "bright". The structure of the character indicates this is a phonogram, composed of 心 as a graphic radical (literally meaning "heart" as ancient people used to believe wisdom rises from one's heart) and 彗 as a phonetic radical.

一	=	三	丰	丰	圭	幸	丰丰
丰丰	彗	彗	彗	彗	彗	慧	

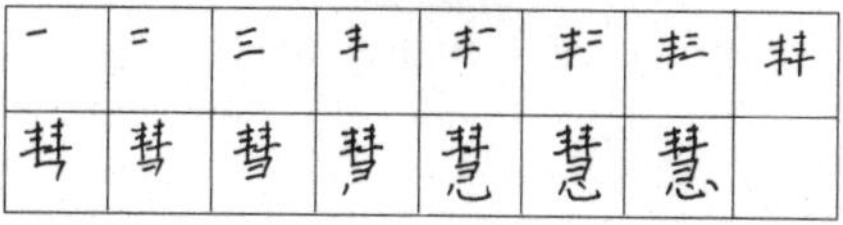

Evolution of form:

In the seal script it is written as 彗 , the two "生"s on top represent a reed broom and the symbol " �ヨ " in the middle indicates a hand. Together they constituted the archaic form of the phonetic radical 彗, meaning "sweep with a broom in the hand." The radical "心" below is the archaic form of 慧 's semantic symbol "心". In the regular script it is written as 慧.

41

Cultural connotation:

The word 慧 indicates "wisdom" and "intelligence." It is often seen in female names, holding the parents' wish for their daughters to be talented. Therefore 慧 sometimes carries a feminine meaning. When you write a letter to a female, you may add "慧鉴"after her name. For example, if you write a letter to Ms Lily Zhou, you may write in a polite and formal form " 周莉丽小姐慧鉴 ".

Frequently used phrases:

智(zhì clever)慧: wisdom

慧眼(yǎn eye): a mind which perceives both past and future; mental discernment insight

聪(cōng wise)慧: bright; intelligent

秀(xiù elegant)外(wài outward; outside)慧中(zhōng in; amidst): beautiful and intelligent

思 Sī think

思 is a verb and it is used for two meanings — one is "to think (over a problem)" and the other meaning is "to long for" or "to miss badly". Both meanings derive from the original structure of the character with the picture of brain on top 囟 and the picture of heart below 心.

43

思

| 丨 | 冂 | 冂 | 田 | 田 |
| 田 | 思 | 思 | 思 | |

Evolution of form:

seal script 🖼 regular script 思

Cultural connotation:

Chinese scholars have always been aware of the significance of thinking and thinking deeply during one's learning period, as Confucius said "**He who learns but does not think is lost** (学而不思则罔)". Although traditional

Chinese education requests a lot of practice and recitation, it is very different from today's rote-learning test-oriented education pattern because the former also stresses the importance of independent deep thinking. If one uses his brain and heart to think, "**new knowledge is gained by reviewing the old** (温故而知新)". A person who likes to take action after mature consideration is wise and prudent.

Frequently used phrases:

思考(kǎo study; investigate): think deeply; ponder over; reflect on

思念(niàn long for): think of; miss

相(xiāng each other)思: lovesick

思想(xiǎng think): thought; idea

思维(wéi thought; thinking): thought; thinking

三(sān three)思而(ér *conjunction*)行(xíng act): look before you leap

仁 rén **benevolence**

仁 is used as a noun meaning "benevolence" and "kind-heartedness". The very original meaning is deciphered from its structure as the character visually represents "between two persons". Since Confucius' time benevolence and kind-heartedness has always been espoused as a virtue in dealing with human relations.

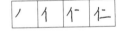

Evolution of form:

In the bone script it is written as 𝕭 . The radical on top symbolizes a person and the two horizontal lines below is the Chinese character of "two". Together they stand for "two persons".

seal script 𝕭 **regular script** 仁

47

Cultural connotation:

One of the key tenets in *The Analects of Confucius* (《论语》) is on the importance of benevolence and kind-heartedness as Confucius once said to his students, **"Benevolence is humanity. (人者仁也)"**. According to his teaching a person in possession of benevolence and kind-heartedness is a great man. An emperor governing a country with benevolence and kindheartedness is loved by his people.

Frequently used phrases:

仁爱(ài love): kind-heartedness; benevolence; humanity

仁慈(cí kind): mercy

仁兄(xiōng elder brother): (polite term to a male friend) my dear friend

仁人(rén person)君子(jūnzǐ gentleman): benevolent gentleman

仁至(zhì extremely)义(yì justice)尽(jìn to the utmost): treat someboby. with the utmost decency and kindness; do everything possible to help

仁者(zhě person)见(jiàn see)仁，智(zhì wise)者 (zhě person)见(jiàn see)智(zhì wise): the benevolent see benevolence and the wise see wisdom — opinions differ from person to person

Do you know?

Five cardinal virtues in traditional Chinese ethics:

仁(rén benevolence)
义(yì justice)
礼(lǐ propriety)
智(zhì wisdom)
信(xìn trustworthiness)

静 jìng quiet

静 is an adjective meaning "still", "quiet" and "calm". 静 is also a phonographic character; its sound goes after the left 青, and its meaning adopts the opposite meaning of the radical on the right.

一	二	丰	圭	丰	青	青
青	青	靑	靜	靜	靜	静

Evolution of form:

In the bronze script it was written as 𩪊, made up of "屮" the phonetic symbol and "𠂇" the semantic symbol. However, this semantic part "𠂇" ("争" in regular script) does not directly correspond to the meaning of the character. "争" means "dispute", in contrast, "静" means "calmness" and "tranquility". Here the semantic part only suggests the category of meaning.

regular script 靜

Cultural connotation:

While Voltaire believes that "Life lies in physical exercise", people in China hold that "still waters run deep (静水流深）". Chinese people may not be as strong as athletes, but have healthy eating habits and a calm and peaceful attitude towards life. Of course being quiet and calm does not mean to be numb; it is an active and wise choice before one is ready to take the next great action. To rest quietly is to recuperate and to contemplate is to free one's mind from anxiety and disturbance. A person who keeps quiet keeps himself away from trouble and rumors. A person who stays calm is capable of handling complex situations.

Frequently used phrases:

安(ān tranquil)静: quiet; peaceful

宁(níng serene)静: tranquil

文(wén refined; mild)静: gentle and quiet

静穆(mù solemn): solemn and quiet

静悄悄(qiāoqiāo quietly): very quiet

风(fēng wind)平(píng calm)浪(làng wave)静: calm and tranquil

智 zhì wisdom

智 is a noun meaning "wisdom", "resourcefulness" and "wit". The left part of the bone script represents a tortuous road 彳; the right part represents a person 亻 and in the middle is the shape of a mouth. Together the character means a person who can find the way on a tortuous road has wisdom.

(Zhuge Liang, Chinese representative figure of wisdom)

54

丿	𠂉	上	牛	矢	知
知	知	智	智	智	智

Evolution of form:

bronze script 𥎦 **seal script** 智

55

Cultural connotation:

Chinese culture has accumulated much wisdom from history. When you carefully read such classics as *Analects* by Confucius, *The Art of War* by Sun Zi and *Records of the Historian* by Sima Qian you can see the wisdom of Chinese people. For Chinese, the most representative figure of wisdom is undoubtedly Zhuge Liang in the Three Kingdoms Period (220-280).

Frequently used phrases:

智力 (lì power; ability): intelligence

智谋 (móu scheme; stratagem): resourcefulness

智勇(yǒng brave)双(shuāng both)全(quán complete):
be both intelligent and courageous

吃(chī suffer; incur)一(yí one)堑(qiàn moat; chasm)，
长(zhǎng gain)一(yí one)智: A fall into the pit, a gain
in your wit.

智者(zhě person)千(qiān thousand)虑(lù think)，必
(bì certainly)有(yǒu have)一(yì one)失(shī lose, miss):
The wisest man, in a thousand schemes, must make at
least one mistake.

Do you know?

Chinese Representative Figure of Wisdom

As a famous military strategist, Zhuge Liang (181-234) won so many battles and accomplished so many missions that were considered impossible that he was always regarded as the representative figure of wisdom. His name as well as his image with a feather fan is widely known among Chinese people.

和 hé **harmony**

和 is a character with many purposes. It is an adjective, a noun, a preposition and a conjunction. When used as an adjective it means "gentle" and "mild"; as a noun it means "harmony" and "peace"; as a preposition it means "with"; and as a conjunction it means "and". Though seemingly a character with many meanings , 和 originally means a kind of reed pipe wind instrument.

和 hé

| 丿 | 二 | 千 | 禾 |
| 禾 | 利 | 和 | 和 |

Evolution of form:

In the bone script it is written as 𤔲, "禾" indicates its sounds, and "口" indicates "using one's mouth", and right symbol "卅" images after the shape of the musical instrument.

bronze script 龢 and 鉌

seal script 和   **regular script** 和

60

Cultural connotation:

China has always been a peace-loving nation. Chinese have an idiom which means "Harmony is what matters (和为贵)". They also believe that peace and harmony bring forth fortune and prosperity. Traditional Chinese families are large, therefore it is important to keep a harmonious atmosphere. It used to be common for three to four generations to live together under one roof . Time has changed. Now the living condition of Chinese citizens, especially those in big cities like Shanghai and Beijng, has improved. However, it is still a popular phenomenon and it is important to cherish and maintain a harmonious relationship within a family, a community or a work unit.

Frequently used phrases:

和好(hǎo friendly; kind): become reconciled

和谐(xié harmony; accord): harmonious

和为(wéi be)贵(guì valuable): Harmony is what matters.

和风(fēng wind)细(xì fine; delicate)雨(yǔ rain): like

, a gentle breeze and light rain—in a gentle and mild way

和气(héqì polite)生(shēng give rise to)财(cái wealth): amiability begets riches (a motto for businessmen)

家(jiā family)和万事(wànshì everything)兴(xīng prevail; prosper): If the family lives in harmony, all affairs will prosper.

Do you know?

和, the Basis of China's Foreign Affairs Policy

和平(hépíng peace)共处(gòngchǔ coexistence)五(wǔ five)项(xiàng *measure word*)原则(yuánzé principle): The Five Principles of Peaceful Co-existence ① mutual respect for territorial integrity and sovereignty ② mutual non-aggression ③ non-interference in each other's internal affairs ④ equality and mutual benefit ⑤ peaceful co-existence

美 měi beautiful

美 is an adjective meaning "beautiful, pretty" and "very satisfactory". 美 is an hieroglyph representing a man dancing 夫 with lots of decorations on head 𠆢 that make his dancing pleasing to the eyes. Over the years 美 developed its meaning from visual beauty to other types of beauty. A song or a dish can also be said to be beautiful.

美 měi

丶	丷	丷	丷	并
美	美	美	美	

Evolution of form:

bone script 笑　　　bronze script 美

seal script 美　　　regular script 美

Cultural connotation:

Though people all over the world have the same un-quenchable pursuit of beauty, the standard of beauty varies. Traditional Chinese esthetical values tend to be delicate and cute in contrast to the western values of great and imposing. A petite figure, cherry-sized mouth, slanting eyes, arched eyebrows, narrow shoulders, small waist and small feet used to be the traditional standards for beautiful Chinese women.

美 měi

Frequently used phrases:

美丽(lì pretty): beautiful

美女(nǚ woman): beautiful woman

美满(mǎn satisfied): happy; very satisfactory

美学(xué subject of study): aesthetics

美食(shí food): delicious food, cuisine

美人(měirén beauty)计(jì stratagem): beauty trap

美中(zhōng in; amid)不足(bùzú deficiency): flaw in something which might otherwise be perfect

Do you know?

Four Great Beauties in China's History

Here are four household names in China: 西施(Xī Shī)，
王昭君(Wáng Zhāojūn)，杨玉环(Yáng Yùhuán,
also known as Yáng Guìfēi, Concubine Yang) and 貂
禅(Diāo Chán). All of them are known to be great
beauties. Among them, Xi Shi ranks first and is always
regarded as the symbol of beauty. Wang Zhaojun is re-
membered both for her beauty and her patriotic spirit
and contribution to strengthen the friendship between
the Han ethic group and the Hsiung-Nu minority in the
Han Dynasty. Yang, the favorite of a Tang Dynasty
emperor, is also known for her dancing and singing talent.

吉祥 jí xiáng **auspicious**

The word 吉祥 means "lucky" and "auspicious". In the ancient time it was written as "吉羊". 吉 originally means "hide the weapons in the box" 🔨, signifying there are no wars or disasters. And sheep in the ancient time was considered a lucky animal just like a phoenix or dragon. Therefore 吉羊 together represents "luck".

68

吉　祥

| 一 | 十 | 士 | 吉 | 吉 | 吉 |

| 丶 | 冫 | ㇇ | ネ | ネ | 衤 |
| 衤 | 衤 | 祥 | 祥 | | |

Evolution of form:

bone script 龠羊　　bronze script 龠羊

seal script 吉羊　　regular script 吉祥

Cultural connotation:

Just like other ancient nations, China with its long history has preserved many old customs and beliefs which serve as a reminder of the old days when people could not explain the mysteries of the world and universe. Things that represent fortune, new life, hope and strength are generally considered lucky and things that are connected with death, sickness and disasters are despised as unlucky. Although to some western scholars this is pure superstition, more and more Chinese people are nostalgic about traditional folklore. They bring forth warmth and comfort in today's increasing rational and mechanical world.

Frequently used phrases:

吉利(lì favorable; smooth): good luck

吉兆(zhào omen): a good omen

吉祥物(wù thing): mascot

吉人(rén person)天(tiān sky; heaven)相(xiàng assist; help): God helps the kind-hearted.

吉星(xīng star)高(gāo high)照(zhào shine; illuminate): The lucky star shines bright.

万事(wànshì everything)大(dà big; great)吉: Everything is just fine.

Do you know?

Auspicious animals: dragon / phonenix / bat / magpie / sheep...

Auspicious plants: pine / bamboo / plum / peony...

Auspicious characters: 福、喜、吉祥、如意、寿······

Auspicious numbers: 6 (means smooth), 8 (means fortune)...

财 cái **wealth**

财 is a noun meaning "money" or "wealth". It is a phonograph with its left part in shell shape 貝 representing wealth and the right part representing its pronunciation.

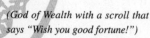

(God of Wealth with a scroll that says "Wish you good fortune!")

财 (財)

一	冂	冂	贝
贝	财	财	

Evolution of form:

The earliest script available is in the seal script in which the character is written as 財.

Cultural connotation:

Money is not always a good thing. On one hand, people want to have more money, therefore on the fifth day of the Lunar New Year they light firecrackers to welcome the God of Wealth. On the other hand, money is known to be a source of evil and greed. In most Chinese mainstream literature, few people are rich and kind at the same time.

Frequently used phrases:

财富(fù wealth): wealth; riches

财主(zhu owner): moneybags (usually with negative personality)

财神(shén god)爷(yé form of address for god): the God of Wealth

财迷(mí bewitch)心窍(xīnqiào aperture of the heart

as a thinking organ): be obsessed by a lust for money

财大(dà big; great)气粗(qìcū overbearing): He who has money speaks louder than others.

财运(yùn luck)亨通(hēngtōng prosper): run a good luck in money transactions

财源(yuán source)滚滚(gǔngǔn come or occur continuously): Wealth keeps rolling in.

Do you know?
You may find it's hard to fall asleep on the fifth night of the lunar New Year in China (especially in Shanghai), because the fireworks are lit all night to welcome the God of Wealth, who they believe will bring fortune to their family.

宝 bǎo **treasure**

宝 is used both as a noun and an adjective. As a noun it means "treasure"; as an adjective it means "invaluable" and "precious". The bone script of this character has a roof on top ⌂, shell ⻌ and an axe ⼯ below. Roof represents home, shell represents money and treasure, and axe represents regime. These are all precious to a family. Later the meaning was extended to refer to all things that are precious.

宝（寶）

| 丶 | 丷 | 宀 | 宀 |
| 宀 | 宇 | 宝 | 宝 |

Evolution of form:

bone script 望   regular script 宝

Cultural connotation:

There is not too much difference in the cultural connotation of this character. Anything precious can be claimed to be 宝 no matter if it is a picture, a book or a brush.

Frequently used phrases:

宝座(zuò seat): throne

宝藏(zàng depository): precious deposits

宝贝(bèi): treasured object; (casual) darling; baby

宝贵(guì valuable): valuable; precious

聚(jù gather)宝盆(pén bowl): treasure bowl—place rich in natural resources

宝刀(dāo knife; sword)不(bù not)老(lǎo old): The man is old but not his sword—one maintains one's strength and skills even as he grows older.

家 jiā **home**

家 is a noun originally meaning "home" as in the bone script it pictures a pig  under a roof representing home. It now also means "a specialist in a certain field", someone who is at home with his profession.

家

丶	宀	宀	宀	宀
宀	豕	豕	豕	家

Evolution of form:

bone script 㝅   bronze script 宀

seal script 家   regular script 家

Cultural connotation:

Chinese people are traditionally very family-oriented. Once a couple gets married, they establish a family and their duty for the rest of their lives is to maintain the well being of the family including raising kids. In Chinese "home" or "family" is the same word. The prosperity of a nation depends on the prosperity of each family. Therefore it is the duty of every patriotic citizen to manage his family well before they are qualified to manage state affairs. Confucius said in the first chapter of *The Great Learning* (《大学》): "**Wishing to order well their States, they first regulated their families.** (欲治其国者，先齐其家). "

Frequently used phrases:

家庭(tíng front yard): family; household

家乡(xiāng native place): hometown

家法(fǎ discipline): domestic discipline exercised by the head of a family

家属(shǔ): family members

家喻(yù know)户(hù family)晓(xiǎo know): known to every household; known to all

家书(shū letter)抵(dǐ balance)万(wàn ten thousand)金(jīn gold): A letter from home is worth ten thousand pieces of gold.

家丑(jiāchǒu family scandal)不可(bùkě should not)外(wài outside)扬(yáng spread): Don't wash your dirty linen in public.

家家有(yǒu have)本(běn *measure word*)难(nán difficult)念(niàn read)的(de *particle*)经(jīng sutra): Every family has some sort of trouble.

孝 xiào   filial piety

孝 is a noun meaning "filial piety". The bone script of this character represents a child supporting an old man. This is the original picture of filial piety.

一	十	土	耂
耂	孝	孝	

Evolution of form:

bone script 孝   bronze script 孝

seal script 孝   regular script 孝

Cultural connotation:

Filial piety is a very important concept in China as Confucius once pointed out "**Filial piety is the source of virtue**. (夫孝，德之本欤。)" In traditional Chinese families parents enjoy absolute superiority over children. Children were obliged to obey and please their parents. Even marriage was decided by their parents. Taking good care of one's parents is the primary task of an adult. The positive side of this tradition is that in China they have great respect for the elderly. And this tradition has been preserved until today.

Frequently used phrases:

孝敬(jìng respect): show filial respect to (one's elders)

孝顺(shùn obey): show filial obedience

孝子(zǐ son; child): a filial son, a dutiful son

孝心(xīn mind; feeling): filial love

尽(jìn try one's best)孝: be filial to one's parents

好 hǎo **good**

好 is a widely used adjective meaning "good". The bone script originally represents a woman 𛰀 with a child 𛰁 at the breast. At that time when only a small percentage of new babies would survive the harsh environment a mother with child is a lucky and definitely a "good" thing.

乚	𡿨	女	女	好	好

Evolution of form:

bone script 𡥈   **bronze script** 𡥈

seal script 𡥈   **regular script** 好

Cultural connotation:

Just like its translation in English the word 好 actually has many meanings according to different uses. Sometimes it means "delicious", sometimes it means "responsible", and sometimes it means "kind".

Frequently used phrases:

好看(kàn look; see): good-looking

好听(tīng hear): pleasant to the ears

好处(chù part; point): benefit

好感(gǎn feeling): favorable impression

花(huā flower)好月(yuè the moon)圆(yuán round): (mostly used as complimentary address for the newly married) blooming flowers and full moon—perfect conjugal bliss

好事(shì thing)成(chéng become; turn into)双(shuāng double): good things come in pairs

好好先生(xiānsheng sir): Mr. Please-all

明 míng **bright**

明 is an adjective that contains a variety of meanings. The original meaning of 明 is "bright" as in " 明月 " (indicating "a bright moon"), the antonym of which is 暗 (àn dark). The original meaning can be seen from the character's structure. As an associative character the archaic form of the character consists of two components — the left part symbolizes the moon and the part on the right is the image of the sun. The original meaning derives from the structure indicating as bright as the sun and the moon. Later the meaning of 明 extends into "clear, distinct" as in " 明白 ", "definite" as in " 明确 ", "wise" as in " 英明 ", "aboveboard, uprightness" as in " 光明磊落 ", etc.

I	⺆	⺁	日
日)	明	明	明

Evolution of form:

In the oracle bone script it is written as ◖日, the left being a symbol ⊂ shaped after 月(moon)and the right being the symbol 日 indicating 日(sun).

bronze script ☉)   **seal script** ◑Ͽ

regular script 明

Cultural connotation:

明 (brightness) and 暗 (darkness) are visible to the most primitive eyes. In the long evolution the meaning of 明 extended beyond its original meaning indicating physical light as opposed to shade. The character 明 embodies "honesty", "aboveboard" and "fair and square" as in 明人不做暗事 (indicating "An honest person doesn't deal under the table."), 明来暗往 (indicating "have covert and overt contacts") and 明辨是非 (indicating "make a clear distinction between right and wrong"). In the feudal courtrooms there usually hangs a stele above the judge which says " 明镜高悬 " — the court is like a bright mirror with which right and wrong is judged with absolute fairness.

Frequently used phrases:

明亮(liàng bright): bright

明白(bai clear): understand

明鉴(jiàn inspect; scrutinize): penetrating judgement

明确(què true; real): clear and definite; clear-cut

明察(chá investigate)暗(àn hidden; secret)访(fǎng seek by inquiry or search): observe publicly and investigate privately

明枪(qiāng spear)易(yì easy)躲(duǒ avoid; dodge), 暗(àn hidden; secret)箭(jiàn arrow)难(nán difficult) 防(fáng guard against): It's easy to dodge a spear thrust in the open, but difficult to guard against an arrow shot from hiding.

明修(xiū build)栈道(zhàndào a plank roadway built along perpendicular rock-faces by means of wooden brackets fixed into the cliff), 暗渡(dù cross)陈仓 (chéncāng an ancient city in Sichuan Province): pretend to advance along one path while secretly going along another — do one thing under cover of another

东 dōng **east**

东, archaically written as 東, originally refers to a bag with both ends bound by ropes. Later the character came to mean "east", depicting a sun rising in the forest.

93

东（東）

Evolution of form:

bone script  **bronze script** 

seal script  (depicting a sun rising just above the horizon but not yet surpassing the crown of the tree)

regular script 、(interchangeable with its simplified version "东")

Cultural connotation:

In ancient China hosts of a big banquet usually sat facing east while the guests sat facing west. For that reason the direction of east has become a symbol of being the host or the boss, hence the words 房东 (fángdōng landlord), 东家(dōngjiā a form of address formerly used by an employee to his employer or a tenant-peasant to his landlord) and 东道主(dōngdàozhǔ host).This tradition has been preserved until today on stately occasions. East has therefore become a respected direction in China.

Frequently used phrases:

做(zuò be; become)东: be the host

东山(shān mountain)再(zài again)起(qǐ brace up): stage a comeback

东施(Dōngshī the name of an ugly woman)效(xiào imitate)颦(pín frown): blind imitation with ludicrous effect

东张(zhāng look; glance)西(xī west)望(wàng look): glance (or peer) around

国 guó country

国, archaically written as 或, is an associative character, depicting the core nature of a country that consists of a piece of land "囗" and weapons "戈", symbolizing soldiers defending the land with weapons. The original meaning of 国, that of country, is still in use today. Besides the meaning of "country", 国 also refers to the kingdoms of princes and vassals as in the name of a classic novel *Romance of Three Kingdoms* (《三国演义》).

Evolution of form:

In the bone script 国 is written as 𢆶, composed of a

" 口 ", symbolizing the land, and a " 戈 ", symbolizing

weapons used to defend the land.

In the bronze script four lines were added to the four

sides of " 口 ", thereby written as 𩱍, further emphasiz-

ing an enclosed land.

seal script 國   **regular script** 國

97

Cultural connotation:

Chinese people understand that the prosperity of a state builds on the well-being of each family. Therefore ancient Chinese rulers tend to relate country to family, just a bigger unit. The emperor is the father of his citizens and it is his duty to govern the country well. The common folk are subject to the royal court the way offspring are to parents. Therefore Chinese people are filled with patriotism, a very strong sense to defend China.

Frequently used phrases:

国宝(bǎo treasure): national treasure

国画(huà painting): traditional Chinese painting

国父(fù father): father of a republic (formerly an epithet for Dr. Sun Yat-sen)

国泰(tài peaceful)民(mín the people)安(ān peaceful): The country is prosperous and the people live in peace.

国计(jì livelihood)民(mín the people)生(shēng livelihood): the national economy and the people's livelihood

国破(pò conquered)家(jiā family)亡(wáng die): country conquered and family ruined

国家(guójiā country)兴亡(xīngwáng rise and fall)，匹夫(pǐfū an ordinary man)有(yǒu have)责(zé responsibility): Every man has a share of responsibility for the fate of his country.

汉 hàn **han**

汉, in its archaic form 漢, originally refers to the Han River, the bigger branch of Yangtze Rive located in Hubei province today. It is a phonogram, the left part " 氵 " indicates a river, and the right radical indicates its sound after " 難 " (the right part " 隹 " is omitted). Later the meaning of 汉 extended to refer to the Han nationality, the Chinese language and its characters or the Han Dynasty (206BC-AD220). Sometimes it also refers to the Milky Way as in the idiom 气冲霄汉 (dauntless; fearless).

Evolution of form:

In the seal script it is written as 㵄, composed of a semantic symbol 水 and a phonetic symbol 𦰩.

In the regular script it has evolved to be 汉, interchangeable with its complicated version 漢.

Cultural connotation:

The Han Chinese make up 92% of the population of China. Therefore, they are the largest ethnic group in the world. The Han culture itself is very old, outdating many European cultures by at least a thousand years. The Han are very wise and diligent people, creating the longest lasting civilization in history. The language of the Han Chinese is the most widely spoken in the world. Commonly referred to as Mandarin Chinese, it is actually a Beijing-based dialect of the Han language. The Han language, in its various dialects, has been the official language of China since the Qin Dynasty, or around 221BC. Mandarin is one of the oldest living languages in the world. The Han have been dominant in China since the founding of the Chinese

Empire, except for two periods totaling about 400 years.
The Mandarin class was mainly made up of Han, as was
the massive bureaucracy power base in the Chinese Empire,
even during the periods when the Han were not in direct
control, such as the Yuan Dynasty (1271-1368) and Qing
Dynasty (1644-1911).

Frequently used phrases:

汉字(zì word; character): Chinese character

汉代(dài dynasty): Han Dynasty

汉语(yǔ language): Chinese (language)

汉族(zú nationality): Han Ethnic Group

汉奸(jiān traitor): traitor (to China)

道 dào **way**

道 was the original form of 导 (導). The original meaning was "to guide the road". It also means "road". The meaning was further extended to "way" or "method". 道 (The Way) is a key word in Taoism. (See *Cultural connotation*).

| 丶 | 丷 | 亠 | 丷 | 丷 | 首 |
| 首 | 首 | 首 | 首 | 道 | 道 |

Evolution of form:

In the bronze script, 道 was written as 𝌀. The outside
"彳亍" (行) symbolizes "road". And the 𝌀 in the middle
depicts a person's head, a symbol of knowing and
guiding. Together the archaic form of the character means
"to guide the road".

seal script 𝌀   **regular script** 道

Cultural connotation:

Both Laozi and Zhuangzi, two prominent figures in the development of Taoism, treat the Way as a key concept. In contrast to the Confucians who used this word to refer to the ethically correct way for humankind, the way of the sages and the true kings, the Taoists used it to refer to the way of nature, a way beyond the full comprehension of human beings, but with which they must seek to accord. Taoists didn't place human beings at the centre of the cosmos and were concerned that human contrivance upset the natural order of things. Rather they affirmed the Way, the indivisible, indescribable, immaterial force of energy that is the source of all that exists or happens. The theories in Taoism are quite abstract and difficult to understand. However, we can see some primitive thoughts of dialectics and anarchism in *Classics of the Way and Its Power* (《道德经》) such as **"When everyone in the world sees beauty in the beautiful, ugliness is already there. When everyone sees good in the good, bad is already** there." and "Keep the people always without knowledge and without desires, for then the clever will not dare act. Engage in no action and order will prevail."

Frequently used phrases:

道德(dé moral): morals; ethics

道家(jiā expert): Taoism (a school of thought in the Spring and Autumn and Warring States Period, 770-221 BC)

道理(li reason; truth): truth; principle

替(tì replace)天(tiān God)行道(xíngdào implement or carry out one's ideas or ideals): implement political ideals in the name of Heaven; do Heaven's bidding

道不同(bùtóng different)，不相为谋(bù xiāng wéi móu there is little common ground for understanding): there is no point in people taking counsel together who follow different ways

气 qì qì

气 is generally translated into "air". It originally referred to "gas" in the physical sense of the world. However in Chinese culture the character 气 bears a further meaning that involves an occult philosophy and Chinese traditional medicine.

气 (氣)

| ノ | ト | ヒ | 气 |

Evolution of form:

In the bone script it is written as 三, similar to the character "Three" (三). It depicts the form of gas in the air.
In the bronze script a small curve was added to its head
and tail 气 to distinguish itself from "Three" (三).
In the seal script it was written as 气, further simplified
and distinct from its original bone script.
In the regular script a 米 was added to become氣.

109

Cultural connotation:

Chinese philosophy developed a unique understanding of 气 in the early days. Ancient philosophers thought it was the basic element in the universe that forms all substances. 气 exists everywhere and all matters derive from it. Therefore 气 has become as important as life itself. People understand it to be the origin of life and vigor. It is the essence, the spirit that survives in a living substance. A painting can not lose its 气 or it loses its attraction. An army can not lose its 气 or it loses its morale. In the same way, a country can not lose its 气 or it falls. When applied in traditional Chinese medicine 气 has become equally important as blood, the loss of which would cause decline and death. Conversely the appropriate application of 气 would produce incredible power and energy, widely known as Chinese *Qigong* (气功).

Frequently used phrases:

气度(dù magnanimity): manner

气质(zhì nature; character): disposition

气韵(yùn appeal; charm): the spirit, character, tone, or style (in the broadest sense) of a work of art or literature

元(yuán chief; principal)气: vitality; vigour

骨(gǔ character; spirit)气: moral integrity

争(zhēng strive)气: try to win credit for; try to make a good showing

气节(jié moral integrity): moral integrity

武 wǔ military

武 is an associative character that consists of a "戈" (indicating a martial weapon in old feudal society) on top and a "止" below that depicts the shape of a human foot. Together the structure of the characters means "ready to take up weapon and set off to the battlefield". The original meaning of 武 is "military". Later it came to mean "valiant" and "fierce".

| 一 | 二 | 干 | 干 |
| 干 | 正 | 武 | 武 |

Evolution of form:

bone script 武   bronze script 武

seal script 武   regular script 武

Cultural connotation:

武 is often used in contrast to 文, the former means "military" and the latter means "literary". It is common knowledge that a state governor needs both military powers and literary management (文治和武治). However, in Chinese history the importance of 武 is always lower than 文. China has always been a peace-loving country and its people are mild in nature. If in the west it was the generals that made history, in China it was the literati that made the history. In *The Book of History* (《尚书》) there is a line that "advocates the importance of literary control of a country and opposes military actions" (偃武修文). Although the safety of a country relies on its strong national defense, it is not the generals that stand on the highest position of the royal court but the literati officials. As a matter of fact there are a lot of generals in the history who prevailed on the battlefield with their valor but died due to the canning of literati officials.

Frequently used phrases:

武官(guān officer): military officer

武器(qì implement): weapon

武力(lì force): military force

武士(shì commendable person): warrior

武术(shù art; skill): martial arts such as shadowboxing, swordplay, etc.

武侠(xiá a person adept in martial arts and given to chivalrous conduct): chivalrous swordsman

龙 lóng **dragon**

龙 means dragon. It is a pictographic character whose meaning hasn't changed since its formation. 龙 is a kind of animal that doesn't exist. It is said to have the head of a camel, the antlers of a deer, the eyes of a rabbit, the ears of a cow, the neck of a snake, the belly of a clam, the scale of carp, the claws of an eagle and the palms of a tiger.

龙 (龍)

一	ナ	尢	龙	龙

Evolution of form:

In the oracle bone script it is written as 瓦, just the depiction of the shape of a dragon.

seal script 龘 **regular script** 龍

Cultural connotation:

Dragons don't exist. It is the product of human imagination. In China people believed it to be the carrier of gods, thus it can soar across heaven. While people in the west regard a dragon as a dreadful totem, Chinese people treat the dragon as a symbol of nobility and fortune and believe themselves to be the descendants of a dragon. Dragon is adopted by virtually all Chinese feudal emperors to identify their superiority. As a matter of fact, the word 龙 has almost become a symbol of royalty. The emperor's bed is called 龙床 (literally "dragon's bed"), and the emperor's son is called 龙子(literally "dragon's son"). The close connection between dragon and royal life has in turn affected the common folk's thoughts. Parents wish their sons to become dragons, a symbol of success and superiority, and their daughters to become phoenix, which always accompanies dragons. (Note: In the feudal royal court, the phoenix was the symbol for the queens and the queen mothers.)

Frequently used phrases:

龙袍(páo robe): emperor's robe

龙眼: (yǎn eye):longan

龙舟(zhōu boat): dragon boat

龙凤(fèng phoenix)呈(chéng assume)祥(xiáng auspicious): The dragon and the phoenix bringing prosperity—excellent good fortune.

龙头(tóu head)产品(chǎnpǐn product): (fig.) flag-ship product

龙争(zhēng compete; vie)虎(hǔ tiger)斗(dòu fight): fierce struggle between evenly-matched opponents

望(wàng hope)子(zǐ son)成(chéng become)龙，望(wàng hope)女(nǚ daughter)成(chéng become)凤(fèng phoenix): long to see one's son become a dragon and daughter become a phoenix (i.e. win success)

竹 zhú **bamboo**

竹 is the name of a plant, namely, bamboo. As a pictograph, 竹 in its very archaic form looked like two plants of bamboo side by side with their leaves drooped. In the ancient times, people used to write characters on the 竹简 (bamboo scroll stringed up by bamboo pieces for writing on), so 竹 sometimes also refers to writing materials as in the phrase 罄竹难书 (meaning "have too many crimes to record").

ノ	ト	ケ	竹	竹	竹

Evolution of form:

bone script 𣐨 (just the image of bamboo)

seal script 𥴩　　**regular script** 竹

Cultural connotation:

Bamboo is one of the four favorite plants along with Chinese plum, orchid and chrysanthemum. The character of bamboo is highly admired by the Chinese people. Bamboo with its unbent trunk and lonely location represents uprightness and seclusion from earthly dust. And the traditional Chinese literati want to be like the bamboo, to pursue its spirit and beauty. There was a well-known literary group in the Wei and Jin Dynasty(265-420) called "Seven Men of Honor in the Bamboos"(竹林七贤). The group members identified themselves with high-heartedness and distinctive talents. They often gathered in bamboo forests near Ji Kang 嵇康(one of the group members)'s home, drank all day long and composed poems to ridicule the royal court and the dark side of society.

Frequently used phrases:

竹林(lín forest): bamboo forest

竹简(jiǎn slip): bamboo slip (used for writing on in ancient times)

成(chéng accomplish)竹在(zài be at, in or on)胸(xiōng mind; heart): have a well-thought-out plan

青(qīng blue or green)梅(méi plum)竹马(mǎ horse): green plums and a bamboo horse — a girl and a boy playing innocently together; a man and a woman who had innocent affection for each other in childhood; puppy love

竹篮(lán basket)打水(dǎshuǐ draw water)一场空(yì cháng kōng all in vain): draw water with a bamboo basket—achieve nothing

梅 méi plum

梅 means "plum", including plum trees, plum blossoms and plum fruits. It is originally written as "某", composed of 木 (indicating it is a plant) and 甘 (a direct depiction of plum blossoms). Later "某" the written form was loaned to use as an indicative pronoun such as 某人 (somebody), 某地 (somewhere) while its sound was preserved and people created another phonogram to take its place. Now the current character 梅 consists of a semantic part "木" and a phonetic part "每".

| 一 | 十 | 才 | 木 | 朴 | 杧 |
| 杧 | 栂 | 栂 | 梅 | 梅 | |

Evolution of form:

In the bone script it was written as 杲. The character depicts the shape of a plum tree with blossoms on top and a trunk below.

In the bronze script people simplified the part on top that symbolizes plum blossoms and doubled the radical. So it changed to its new form 槑.

In the seal script people wrote in the new phonogram form 楳.

In the regular script the written form of the character is fixed into 梅.

梅 méi

Cultural connotation:

Plum ranks first among the "Four Elegant Flowers" (花中四君子) followed by orchid, bamboo and chrysanthemum. It blooms against intense coldness, hence it is also referred to as one of the "Three Plant Friends Thriving in the Cold"(岁寒三友) together with pine and bamboo. Plum is commonly used by ancient poets as a metaphor for fortitude, uprightness, strong will and clear conscience. Plum is also praised for not contending with other flowers when spring comes, a quality pursued by people not willing to become deeply involved in worldly affairs. The great patriotic poet Lu You (陆游) in the Song Dynasty (960-1279) once wrote "Beside the broken bridge and outside the post-hall, a flower is blooming forlorn. Saddened by her solitude at nightfall, by wind and rain she's further torn. Let other flowers their envy pour. To spring she lays no claim. Fallen in mud and ground to dust, she seems no more. But her fragrance is still the same." More than seven hundred years later the great leader Chairman Mao Zedong countered Lu's poem with his *Ode to the Plum Blossom* (《卜算子·咏梅》), "Then spring departed in wind and rain; With flying snow it's back again. Though icicles from beetling cliffs still hang miles long, one flower sweet and fair is there among. Though sweet and fair, with other flowers she won't rival, but only heralds spring's arrival. When mountain flowers run riot for miles and miles, among them she will be all smiles."

Frequently used phrases:

梅花(huā flower): plum blossoms

梅雨(yǔ rain): plum rain

话(huà)梅: preserved plum

腊(là twelfth lunar month)梅: wintersweet

梅花(huā flower)鹿(lù deer): sika (deer)

棋 qí chess

棋, also translated to "chess" in modern understanding, actually refers to "I-go" (围棋) instead of Orthodox Chess in traditional Chinese. The character 棋 is also written as 棊. 棋 is a phonogram, consisting of a semantic symbol 木, indicating that chess are made of wood, and a phonetic symbol 其.

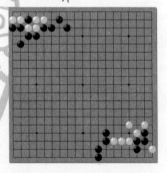

一	十	扌	木	朾	村	柑
柑	柑	棋	棋	棋		

Evolution of form:

The early day forms of 棋 were lost but it can be certain that in the regular script it has evolved to become 棋.

Cultural connotation:

I-go was believed to be invented by legendary Emperor Yao (尧帝) . In the early days 棋(I-go) was invented as a pragmatic game associated with war drills and strategies. The close connection is reflected in its rules. However by the time of Spring and Autumn Periods (770BC-476BC) it had become prevalent as an elegant game for leisure enjoyment. It is often mentioned along with the rest of Four Traditional Arts that an educated Chinese gentleman or lady should possess, namely, 琴 (music), 书(calligraphy) and 画 (brush painting). Many of the great emperors, generals, ministers and literati are masters of the game.

Frequently used phrases:

下(xià play board games)棋: play chess

象(xiàng)棋: chess

棋子(zǐ something small and hard): chessman; piece (in a board game)

棋逢(féng meet)对手(duìshǒu match; equal): meet one's match in a game of chess — be well-matched in a contest

棋高(gāo advanced; superior)一(yì one)着(zhāo move in chess): be superior to one's opponent (in chess or otherwise); outmatch one's opponent

举(jǔ raise; lift)棋不定(búdìng indefinite; indeterminate): hesitate about or over what moves to make

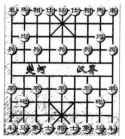

(In Chinese chess, there are 32 pieces, 16 black and 16 red. Each group is composed of 1 commander, 2 guards, 2 prime ministers, 2 canons, 2 horses, 2 chariots and 5 soldiers.)

茶 chá **tea**

茶 is the official name for "tea". 茶 was written as 荼 before the Mid-Tang Dynasty but later with its increased usage in daily writing, a horizontal line was taken from the character to become today's 茶. The word for tea or tea leaves in many languages are derivatives from the Chinese pronunciation.

一	十	艹	艹	艾
苂	苓	荼	茶	

Evolution of form:

茶 was written in its present form since Mid-Tang times.
Before that it was written to be 荼.

Cultural connotation :

Of the three major beverages of the world — tea, coffee and cocoa — tea is consumed by the largest number of people. China is the home of tea. It is believed that China had tea-shrubs as early as five to six thousand years ago, and human cultivation of teaplants dated back two thousand years. Tea from China, along with her silk and porcelain, began to be known in the world over more than a thousand years ago and has since always been an important export. Chinese tea may be classified into five categories according to the different methods by which it is processed. They are green tea, black tea, Wulong tea, compressed tea and scented tea.

Frequently used phrases:

茶杯(bēi cup): tea-cup

茶馆(guǎn a certain service establishments): tea-house

茶叶(yè leaf): tea; tea leaves

茶壶(hú kettle): teapot

茶话(huà talk)会(huì meeting): a tea party at which the participants chat or give talks

粗(cū plain)茶淡(dàn tasteless)饭(fàn meal): plain tea and simple food; homely meal

茶余(yú after)饭(fàn meal)后(hòu after): over a cup of tea or after a meal — at one's leisure

茶饭(fàn meal)不(bù not)思(sī wish; desire): have no appetite

食 shí food

食 is an associative character that means "to eat". It consists of two components with the top part like that of a person's mouth wide open and the bottom part symbolizing rice in the bowl. It also means "to be eaten", 食 as a noun also refers to "food" and "meal".

| ノ | 人 | 人 | 今 | 今 |
| 仝 | 倉 | 食 | 食 | |

Evolution of form:

In the bone script 食 is written 𠊊, the bottom symbol 𣪘 depicts a container of rice and the symbol on top 𠆢 depicts a person eating with his mouth.

bronze script 𣩍 **seal script** 𩚁 **regular script** 食

Cultural connotation:

Food is essential to Chinese people's daily life as the saying goes **"Food is heaven and god to the common folk."** (民以食为天) Thus for many years to eat well is a common aspiration for Chinese people who invented various ways to cook and eat. Chinese food is one of the most delicate cuisines in the world. As a result to understand the importance of Chinese food with its infinite variability has become an important part in understanding Chinese culture. There are eight major styles of Chinese cuisine, namely, Canton Cuisine, Sichuan Cuisine, Shandong Cuisine, Jiangsu Cuisine, Anhui Cuisine, Zhejiang Cuisine, Fujian Cuisine and Hunan Cuisine. Among them Canton and Sichuan Cuisine are most famous, with the former characterized by multiple materials and the latter featured by its spicy flavor.

Frequently used phrases:

食品(pǐn article; product): food

粮(liáng grain; food)食: food

食堂(táng hall or room): canteen

丰(fēng rich)衣(yī clothing)足(zú adequate)食: have ample food and clothing

食不(bù not)果腹(guǒfù satisfy or appease one's hunger): have not enough food in one's belly; go hungry

废(fèi abandon)寝(qǐn sleep)忘(wàng forget)食: (so absorbed or occupied as to) forget all about food and sleep

食不(bú not)厌(yàn be satisfied)精(jīng refined; essential)，脍(kuài finely sliced meat or fish)不(bú not)厌(yàn be satisfied)细(xì fine): be particular about one's food

食之(zhī it)无味(wúwèi tasteless)，弃(qì throw away)之(zhī it)可惜(kěxī a pity): hardly worth eating but not bad enough to throw away

鼎 dǐng **tripod**

鼎 is a kind of vessel used in the archaic times to cook and contain food and drink. It was often made from bronze, featured by its bulk size and tripod.

l	⌐	月	月	目	怘	昗
昗	昗	昗	昗	昗	鼎	

Evolution of form:

In the bone script it is written as 昗 , depicting the shape
of a typical 鼎.

bronze script 昗 **seal script** 鼎 **regular script** 鼎

Cultural connotation:

鼎 was initially invented to be a cooking vessel, however people used it to contain sacrifices in national rituals because of its bulk and imposing shape. Gradually 鼎 has become a symbol of solemnity and thus of great religious importance. In one legendary version the great Emperor Yu of the Xia Dynasty cast nine 鼎 to symbolize the nine states under his rule. He placed the nine 鼎 in the middle of his country. Later 鼎 has acquired a further political emblem of a country. When Emperor Chengtang conquered the Xia dynasty, he moved the nine 鼎 to the new capital of Shangyi. It is noticeable that 鼎 as a cooking vessel and food container was only used by the nobility. Therefore 鼎 is also a symbol of a noble and rich life. The most distinctive feature of 鼎 are the three legs, which is often used as a metaphor for triumvirate and tripartite confrontation.

Frequently used phrases:

鼎立(lì stand): (of three antagonists confronting one another) stand like the three legs of a tripod

鼎盛(shèng prosperity): in a period of great prosperity; at the height of power and splendor

鼎鼎(dǐngdǐng grand; magnificent)大(dà great)名 (míng name): famous

一(yì one)言(yán word)九(jiǔ nine)鼎: decisive word

鼎力(lì strength; effort)相助(xiāng zhù help): make unstinting effort to help somebody